The Tasks of the Trade Unions
First Prism Key Press Edition 2012


Prism Key Press
New York, NY 10001
PrismKeyPress.com


ISBN-13: 978-1475029482

# The Tasks of the Trade Unions

Georgi Dimitrov

# CONTENTS

# The Trade Unions in the Past

The trade unions sprang up during the early stage of capitalism as an organization aimed at improving the economic conditions of the workers within the *framework* of the existing capitalist system. At first they considered it as their task to fight only the individual capitalists in defence of the immediate professional workers' interests, without affecting the foundations of capitalist exploitation and without going beyond the pale of the capitalist industrial social organization.

The abolition of competition among workers of a given trade, the restricted access of new workers to it and the resorting in extreme cases to strikes - those were the usual methods used by the old trade unions in order to obtain higher wages, shorter working hours and better working conditions.

Failing to see the direct tie-up which exists between the condition of the workers in production and the political and state organization of capitalist society, those trade unions, a classical example of which we find in the former British trade unions, shut themselves up in their narrow professional shell, assiduously avoiding all participation in political battles and in the nation's politics in general, and confining themselves to questions pertaining to their trade. This, of course subsequently did not prevent them from being quite frequently used, directly or indirect for the political ends of the bourgeoisie.

In spite of this innocuous character of the first trade unions the bourgeoisie and its state opposed them vehemently and tried by violence, repression and legalized bans to destroy them, sensing instinctively that they might develop into dangerous class organizations, into organs of the class struggle of the proletariat for the abolition of the capitalist system.

The rabid acts of violence, repressions and bans against the trade unions, however, far from failed to produce the result expected by the bourgeoisie. A product of the very development of capitalism, having emerged in the struggle between capital and labour and having become a vital necessity for the workers in their defence against capitalist exploitation, the trade unions could not possibly be eradicated. The persecutions against them only intensified the existing class contradictions in capitalist society and revealed them more clearly to the masses of workers. Without the intervention of the trade unions, the strikes were more frequent, spontaneous and turbulent, inflicting immeasurable damage on production, threatening often even the personal safety and property of individual capitalists.

It was precisely this that finally compelled the bourgeoisie to get *reconciled* to the existence of trade unions, while attempting to *tame* them and to turn them into organizations which would regulate relations between workers and capitalists and maintain a lasting peace in industry.

The British bourgeoisie, which for long was complete master on the international market and owned the largest and richest colonies in the world, had ample possibilities, for the attainment of this goal, to mete out certain material benefits to the trade unions which comprised mainly skilled workers, the so-called *labour aristocracy.*

This marked the beginning of the era of collective contracts, concluded between the trade unions and the capitalist organizations and by fixing by mutual consent the conditions and rates of wages and working time, thereby removing for a long time the *danger of strikes* at the enterprises and in the branches of industry affected by these collective contracts. The well-known *wage scales* were established, according to which wage rates were determined in accordance with the average price of prime necessities over a given period, the calculation, however, being usually so made as to keep wages at the lowest possible level. And in order to involve the workers and their trade unions more deeply in capitalist production, to harness them to it and make them eager collaborators of the capitalists in expending and stabilizing it so as to increase capitalist profit to the utmost, many enterprises resorted to profit-sharing schemes in the form of certain percentages and bonuses granted to the workers. Thus, the capitalists secured a maximum labour efficiency on the part of the workers, safeguarded themselves against their strikes, pocketed fat profits, while all that the workers got was the illusion of participating in the profits of the enterprises and, if what they cot was inadequate, of attributing it not to capitalist exploitation, not to the greed of the capitalists, not to the capitalist system of production itself and the way the goods produced were distributed, but to their own inadequacy in work, to their failure to put in the necessary efforts for the success of production.

Adopting this industrial policy towards the workers, the capitalists strove to make them believe that an improvement of their condition could be achieved not through strikes, not through a struggle against capitalist exploitation, but *solely* through an increase of capital, through an expansion of production, through constantly growing capitalist profits.

And the majority of trade unions in Great Britain and in several other countries, from bodies for the defence of the workers' interests and for fighting capitalism, were turned into Vehicles for the establishment of equilibrium and peace in capitalist production and into an instrument of the nation's capitalists whereby to keep the workers' masses in a state of subordination and bondage, to divert them from the road of the class proletarian struggle and ever to oppose them to the emancipatory workers' revolution.

And when in the middle of the last century, after the founding of the First Socialist International [1] and the

9

publication of the *Communist Manifesto* by Marx and Engels, the proletariat began rapidly to organize itself as a *class of its own* and the trade union movement increasingly adopted Marx's view to the effect that trade unions should not confine themselves to a partisan war against individual capitalists and to the Sisyphean task of lopping off the *branches* without touching the *trunk of* capitalist exploitation but should become *schools of socialism* and strive to abolish capitalism itself by playing a *prime role* in the civil *war* for its downfall, the bourgeoisie adopted a long-term and systematic policy of bribing and corrupting the trade union leaders and the numerous trade union bureaucracy, in order to keep the trade union movement under its influence.

In its press it flattered the trade union leaders as being intelligent and talented workers' representatives, enticed them to come to its sumptuous banquets, courted them in various ways, granted them all sorts of benefits, helped them to enter parliament and kept them firmly in its hands.

It must be admitted that in this way the bourgeoisie quite often succeeded in attaining its goal and in keeping many of the trade unions under its direct or indirect control, of which circumstance it made the widest possible use, in particular during the World War.

# The Trade Unions during the War

Standing on the positions of their nation's capitalists, the majority of British trade unions, the oldest and strong-est trade union organizations, saw in the war the *only* means whereby industry in Great Britain would be able to pre-serve its dominant position on the world market now threat-ened by rising and aggressive German capitalism, and to maintain its sway over India and the other rich colonies, which supplied it with raw materials and vast markets for its products.

And the British trade unions placed themselves at the complete service of the imperialist and bellicose policy of their own bourgeoisie. They attempted to stop all strikes, prolonged the expiring terms of all collective contracts and strove to ensure the widest possible development of the war industry. They gave a great number of volunteers from among their midst and opened special offices for the recruitment of volunteers for the British Army and, when compulsory military service was introduced in Great Britain where it had never existed in the past, they not only did not oppose it, but even enthusiastically applauded this initiative of Lloyd George's as a 'fine' means of forever crushing 'Prussian militarism.'

The German trade unions, on their part, headed by the notorious social-traitor Legien and by the numerous staff of the corrupt workers' bureaucracy, announced that the war of German imperialism against 'perfidious Albion' (England) was at the same time a war for the existence of the working class in Germany, that if the latter were defeated in this war, even the few colonies which she possessed corn pared with Great Britain would be taken away from her, that German industry would be deprived of the raw materials which it needed, its roads to the international markets would be blocked and it would be brought to complete disaster and, together with it, the working class would be reduced to utter misery and unprecedented pauperism and Germany - as Lenin liked to put it - 'instead of exporting goods, would be exporting *live men* its manpower.'

The General Trade Union Committee [2] addressed an ardent appeal to the workers in industry and in the Army, urging them to give their all-round support to 'the sacred defensive war' of Kaiser Wilhelm [3] and the German imperialists, and demanding of the trade unions to make the workers refrain from all strikes, especially in the field of mining and the war industries.

That is how 'civil peace' between the working class and the imperialist bourgeoisie was solemnly proclaimed. At the very moment when the German capitalists and their joint-stock companies were pocketing billions of profits, when the gold rain of the war was pouring into their safes, the German proletarians were shedding their blood on the battlefields or working day and night in industry for the 'defence of the fatherland', while their trade unions *invested* their millions in cash (collected over decades in workers' pennies for fighting capitalist exploitation) *in state loans to finance the perfidious war.*

Accompanying the singing of the rabid hymn of the German imperialists and militarists 'Deutschland, Deutschland fiber alles', [4] the big trade union leaders published a special book, containing articles by the secretaries of the various unions who, with figures relating to their production branches, endeavoured to prove the necessity of Germany's holding Out to the end in the war and of her ernerging as complete victor, proudly declaring that this would inevitably he achieved, because the war on the part of Germany was *a war which the working class was waging for its existence and its future happiness.* They enthusiastically- painted the bright prospects of

12

a military victory for the German workers who would be able freely to travel around the whole world, receiving high wages and enjoying the greatest prosperity!...

At the same time Gompers's AFL [5] was carrying on a very intensive propaganda for America's intervention in the war and, when this intervention became a fact, mobilized all its forces in the service of the American millionaires and corporations.

Even the French trade unions which, under the influence of anarcho-syndicalism [6], were considered extreme and irreconcilable enemies of capitalism, in their bulk committed themselves, for similar reasons, to the service of French financial capital in the war, furled their banners and wholeheartedly embraced the policy of 'civil peace'.

Without dwelling on the betrayal of the trade unions in the other belligerent nations, except for those in Russia, Italy, Bulgaria, Serbia and Rumania which remained completely loyal to the working class and to international proletarian solidarity, we can boldly assert today that if the capitalists in the two warring blocs were able to kindle the holocaust of the world war and drive their peoples into it, if they succeeded in manifesting such titanic forces during its four-year duration, this was due primarily to the fact that they, managed in good time to win over the trade unions which had a membership of many millions to their imperialist cause, and place them at the service of their military policy of conquest.

The old opportunism and auto-syndicalism in the trade union movement; the policy of confining their activity to reforms within the capitalist system; the professional narrow-mindedness, short-sightedness and corruption of the trade union bureaucracy; the education of the workers' masses in the trade unions in a spirit of petty, momentary gains along the road of mutual understanding with the capitalists - all this developed and was brilliantly manifested during the war in the form of a *labour imperialism* which rent asunder the international solidarity of the proletariat and turned the workers in the different countries into deadly enemies who killed each other for the cause of their common enemy - *world capital*.

This, however, proves the complete bankruptcy of the dominant opportunist policy in the trade union movement in most countries, laying bare before the world proletariat and its workers' organizations with absolute clarity the only salutary road - *the road of intransigent class struggle*, along which, we are glad to say, our own trade unions have been undeviatingly marching from the day of their foundation until today.

# Results of the Trade Union Struggle

With the trade methods of struggle, the unions in the different countries did, indeed, achieve quite a few results. The despotic arbitrariness of the boss towards the workers at the enterprises was *restricted*. The workers won the right to intervene, through their trade unions, in the settlement of relations between labour and capital. A rise in the *average* wage level was also obtained as compared with the worker's former exceedingly miserable conditions, as well as shorter working hours, which in the past the capitalists could freely prolong to the physically utmost possible limits.

Moreover, the sums spent by the trade unions during periods of unemployment not only alleviate the heavy lot of the unemployed, but also help to avoid intense competition between unemployed and employed, thus preventing a lowering of wages and the former unrestricted deterioration of general working conditions.

Of course, the benefits derived from the struggle of the trade unions usually go to the skilled and semi-skilled workers, who are those precisely in a position to establish strong trade unions, while the mass of unskilled, general workers enjoy, these benefits but little.

How insignificant, in general however, are the results obtained by trade unions over many years of effort and struggle can be clearly seen from the fact that even in the most highly developed capitalist countries, such as Great Britain, Germany and America, the wage rates prior to the war always ranged about the *minimum* necessary for the workers' elementary sustenance, while the working day in most branches of industry was ten, and only here and there eight hours.

The gains of the trade union struggle are, moreover, not only *insufficient* from the viewpoint of the material, cultural and spiritual needs of the working class; they are also *precarious*.

The capitalists have at their disposal various means of *counteracting* the efforts of the trade unions, aimed at improving labour conditions, as well as at *divesting* them of the fruits of their struggle. The general policy of the state, as well as of the conditions in which capitalist production is developing, facilitates their task in this respect.

Thus, they take advantage, above all, of the possibilities offered them by technical progress, introducing and extending the use of women and children in production. These, owing to their smaller power of resistance and lower susceptibility to organization, usually compete with the adult workers and tend to depress working conditions.

For the same purpose the capitalists use the workers from the backward regions and countries whose culture is lower, as well as the helpless arid ruined urban and rural petty bourgeois who, owing to their restricted means, are ready to work on terms inferior to those which the trade unions have won.

Compelled to reduce the working day, the capitalists now manage to draw from the workers, even during the shorter working hours, as much of their vital force as before, through piece work and the different special systems of utilizing *every movement* of the worker's body while he is at work. A case in point is the well-known American system, known as the Taylor system, which, however, inevitably leads to the rapid physical degeneration of workers and to a shortening of their capacity for work.

Finally, what the trade unions manage to gain through their professional struggle in the way of higher wages, is by and large taken away from them the next moment as a consequence of the general capitalist policy and, in particular, the introduction and increase of indirect taxes, of import duties and a number of similar means which tend to raise the cost of living.

All these special conditions of trade union struggle have long ago suggested to the more advanced and farsighted elements among the working class that this struggle should net be waged in an *isolated* way, that it should be *co-ordinated* with the general political struggle of the proletariat, that a *strike* in production should be combined with the *ballot* and the struggle in parliament, as well as with all forms of mass workers' action, that in a word, the *trade union struggle become a component of the entire class struggle of the proletariat.*

And indeed, wherever this has been applied in practice, the trade union struggle has been more successful and surer. BLit, to be true to historical truth, it must be admitted that, even when the struggle of the trade unions is thus combined, *it's limits* and *chances of success* do not change substantially. Even then, its results, though substantially greater and surer, still remain *insufficient* and *precarious.* They do not create for the working class in capitalist society the possibility of living well and like cultured men, nor do they even substantially decrease the material and social misery in which it lives.

All improvements obtained through *strikes*, on the one hand, and through *labour protection laws*, on the other, as long as political power is in the hands of the bourgeoisie, cannot exceed the limits of a given amount of capitalist profit, as otherwise the very existence of capitalist industry ,would be impossible.

Surveying today the whole history of the struggle of the trade unions, we can see that its only *essential and lasting* result consists in that the workers have *succeeded in resisting the utter exhaustion of their vital forces and in safeguarding themselves against utter physical and moral degeneration to which capitalism is irresistibly pushing them.* The trade unions, however, are not in a position to impose *sufficient and lasting* improvement which would enable the workers' masses to lead a more cultural and happier life *for a long period.*

# The New Conditions of Trade Union Struggle

The World War created conditions which further impede the struggle of the trade unions and substantially lower even the chances of obtaining practical results which it had prior to the war.

First of all, it nullified most of the previous gains in the working conditions of all the belligerent, and even of neutral nations. Everywhere wages far from correspond to the colossal rise in the cost of living. There is a precipice between the *nominal* and the *real* wage, i. c. its actual purchasing power. There is an unprecedented rise in the price of the necessities of life and a shortage of them, an acute housing crisis and unprecedented misery for the working masses in the defeated as well as in the victorious countries.

Moreover, the war radically upset all economic life. For four years, almost 45 million people, instead of producing goods, were engaged in a terrible holocaust of destruction. More than 20 million producers of goods left their lives on the battlefields or were disabled, i.e. deprived of their former capacity for work. Flourishing regions in the world were devastated. All reserves of raw materials and foods were swallowed up by the greedy war monster. Vast spaces of land remained uncultivated. Three-quarters of the farm animals were killed. The workers who returned from the battlefields are physically exhausted and morally upset Trade has been completely disorganized. The former relations between the different economic and industrial regions for the exchange of raw materials and finished goods have been discontinued. The means of communication (railroad, shipping and other communications) have been worn out, etc.

As a result of this disorganization of economic life, many branches of industry today are. at a standstill, and others have altogether ceased to function. Mass unemploy-ment is assuming unprecedented proportions in all countries ofthe world.

Today, in the period of liquidation of the World War, which in effect is no liquidation at all but merely a passing over of the war into *another stage* - into the stage of all imperialist war against the rising international proletarian revolution, capitalism has proved *incapable* of securing peace among nations, of restoring production and securing the elementary survival of the masses. Crushed by the weight of its insoluble internal contradictions, its only *concern* now is to save itself from the revolution, resorting for this purpose to civil war and thereby fanning still further the chaos in production and economic fife and infinitely increasing the sufferings of its own people.

On the other hand, the World War irretrievably ushered in the epoch of the international proletarian revolution. We see its beginning flow in Soviet Russia. The revolutionary movements which have already started in Germany, Austria and Hungary, as well as the intensified undercurrents in Italy, France and Great Britain, whose echo reaches our ears from time to time, testify to its early spread to other countries as well.

Anarchy in economic life, disorganization in production accompanied by mass unemployment and misery are still further heightened by the civil war, whereby the bourgeoisie is trying in vain. to retain its shaken supremacy.

There are no longer any prospects for a return to prewar conditions. The war itself accelerated and revealed the *complete bankruptcy* of the capitalist system of production and trade, of social organization and state government.

History now confronts working mankind with the dilemma: *either to pass over to new forms of production and social organization or to perish under the regime of imperialist barbarity.* The restoration of economic life today is possible only *along socialist lines,* i.e. without the capitalists and *against* them.

But precisely under these new conditions, the efforts of the trade unions to improve the conditions of the workers even back to the pre-war level have become quite *hopeless* and *helpless.* Within the *framework* of the capitalist system this is *excluded.* For its attainment, the first condition to *break* and *go beyond* this framework.

And indeed, how will the trade unions be able to obtain the improvements needed by the workers when economic life today is so upset, when there is such mass unemployment and when the strong and extremely obdurate financial capitalists, whom the war even in our small backward country, raised to the position of absolute rulers and lords in economic life, are inclined to see in every movement for higher wages and shorter working hours a *revolutionary action,* aimed directly at the overthrow of capitalist rule? What labour laws of a nature to expand and consolidate the gains of the trade union struggle could be enacted by the present-day bourgeois state, which is writhing under billions of war debts and is financially bankrupt?

It is, precisely these peculiar conditions in the trade union struggle at the present-day imperialist stage of capitalism which confront the proletariat and, in particular, its trade unions with the immediate task of *doing away with the capitalist system and the ensuing exploitation of labour.*

The moment is setting in when instead of endeavouring through the trade union struggle *slowly and gradually* to improve the workers' condition within the limits of capitalist production, production *itself* has to pass into the hands of the proletariat so as to be organized not for capitalist profit and in favour of a minority, as it is today, but to meet the needs of the working majority and for the general prosperity, of those who work.

# The Struggle for political Power

But it is precisely, for this reason that at the present historical moment the struggle for political power by the proletariat *comes to the fore* and all other efforts and tasks of the workers' organizations, including the trade unions, must be co-ordinated with this struggle and be completely subordinated to it. For the replacement of one social and production system by another is possible only by means of political power. The abolition of capitalist exploitation, which is today the immediate task of the trade unions, can be achieved only if the proletariat wrests power from the hands of the ruling bourgeoisie and establishes a proletarian dictatorship exercised by the workers' councils.

But if the *strike* is the strongest weapon of the trade unions for gaining improvements in production, now, when it is a question of seizing political power and proceeding to a radical reconstruction of production and society, not the *strike*, even in the form of a mass political strike, will settle the issue, but the *proletarian revolution.*

Instead of a struggle with *hands crossed* by different groups and the masses of workers, we have to have a struggle waged by the whole proletariat, which it will terminate with *arms in hand*!

To rally the masses, to educate arid prepare them for this struggle, while they themselves take a most active part in it under the leadership of the Communist Party, *is today the foremost task* of the trade unions, if they wish to remain true to the interests of the proletariat and to their own role of class proletarian organizations.

# Trade Union Neutrality

In this factual and historical state of affairs, is it necessary to prove in detail that there is no room today for any so-called political neutrality - the neutrality of the trade unions with regard to political parties and political struggles?

Trade union neutrality has always been a purely bourgeois idea. Under the guise of political neutrality, the bourgeoisie and its agents in the workers' movement (the right-wing socialists and the various 'workers' friends' arid social-reformers) have attempted to detach the trade unions from the class struggle of the proletariat and turn them into tools for the maintenance of capitalist rule.

In fact, *never* and in no *country* have the trade unions been neutral. The whole history of the workers' movement bears this out. The trade unions have always either remained true to the proletarian cause and have resolutely fought against capitalism, taking part in some way or other in the political struggles in favour of the proletariat, or have directly or indirectly, in one form or another, been at the service of the bourgeoisie, letting the bourgeois parties use them in their internecine struggles for the plums derived from power, and often even in their fight against the emancipatory movement of the proletariat itself

What in fact the neutrality of the trade unions amounts to was best seen during the World War, when the 'neutral' and 'free' trade unions in Germany, France, Great Britain and America committed their treason towards the cause of proletarian liberation, by taking part with might and main in the bellicose imperialist policy of their own Capitalist classes.

And indeed, call the trade unions be *neutral* in the struggle between labour and capital, in which by their very nature they are directly involved?

Still less is it possible today, when class contradictions have reached their peak, when the bourgeoisie and the proletariat are pitted against each other as *class* against class, when the period of the international proletarian revolution has been ushered in, to speak about trade union neutrality.

For the trade unions to be *neutral* today towards the political class party of the proletariat means for them to be *dependent* on the bourgeoisie and to be serving some of bourgeois parties.

For the trade unions to be *neutral* to the workers' revolution which is being implemented means that they will be *helping* the bourgeois counter-revolution.

Either with labour - *against* capital; or with *capital* against *labour*! Either on the side of the *revolution*, or in tile camp of the *counter-revolution*!

*There is no* middle road!

And in this connexion the *form* in which this takes place is of absolutely no significance; what counts is the essence of the matter The fact that certain trade unions are *formally* considered as *neutral* and *independent* means absolutely nothing in fact they cannot be such, and will inevitably go either to the *one* or to the *other* side, to the *one* or to the *other* of the two fighting camps.

The historical development of the proletarian class struggle has not only refuted all bourgeois fallacies about trade union neutrality and independence towards the political organization and struggle of the proletariat, but also imposes today a *still closer unity* between the trade unions and the Communist Party, a *complete organic unity* between the professional and political struggles of the proletariat for *the overthrow of capitalism, the setting up of a proletarian dictatorship and the achievement of communism.*

# The New Tasks of the Trade Unions

The example set to us by Soviet Russia where the proletariat has now been exercising its dictatorship for a year and a half and is implementing the country's socialist reconstruction, has shown clearly that the trade unions do not end their historical role and do not cease to exist even when the proletariat has succeeded, through its revolution in seizing political power. On the contrary, precisely during this *transitional* period of proletarian dictatorship - from the overthrow of the bourgeoisie to the achievement of communism - the trade unions are called upon to play no less important role. Of course, their role now is profoundly different from what they were doing in the period of capitalist production and under bourgeois rule. Here they cease to be organizations of the proletariat against capitalist exploitation, because the capitalists have been removed from production or have been rendered absolutely harmless under the regime of proletarian dictatorship.

True, during this transitional period the trade unions will again continue to defend the workers, but no longer through *strikes* but through the organized influence of *Soviet power.* Together with the proletariat, the *trade unions* themselves, as it were, *have come to power* i.e. become *part* of the government, organs of *Soviet government.*

The trade unions will further have to organize the control and distribution of the work force in the different branches of production, under the general plan worked out by the Soviet Government for the whole nation's economy.

In agreement with the Soviet economic bodies, tile trade

unions will be settling questions referring to the wages and conditions of workers in the different enterprises, will maintain labour discipline in them and work for a maximum increase in labour productivity.

The elaboration of the laws, the fixing of working hours wages, hygienic working conditions, against employment accidents, sickness, old age, etc., as well as the application of these laws will be another important function of the trade unions.

Theirs will also he the task of taking care of general and professional education, necessary for the training of a numerous workers' technical intelligentsia, without which neither the complete regulation of production, nor its nationalization and subsequent organization along socialist lines is conceivable.

And, most important of all, the trade unions will be charged with the task of organizing the *workers' control* over production which will exist until complete socialization is achieved, and of taking into their own hands, as organs of Soviet rule, in conjunction with the other economic bodies, tile organization and management of production and the country's entire economic life.

After the conquest of political power by the proletariat, the trade unions will transfer the centre of their activity to the sphere of the organization of economic life. They will have to prepare the proletariat for the role of organizer of production in the transition from *private capitalist monopoly to state monopoly, and from the latter to the socialist organization of economic life and to complete communism.*

It will be no exaggeration if we say that without the accomplishment of these exceedingly important tasks oil the part of trade unions, *neither a complete nor lasting triumph of the workers' revolution is possible, nor the achievement of communism.*

# Conclusion

The functions of the trade unions prior to the revolution, during the revolution, as well as afterwards during the period of proletarian dictatorship - so important and so complex - imperatively demand that the Bulgarian trade unions become genuine *mass* organizations in composition and in their ties with the broad workers' masses, restoring the *complete* trade union *unity*, and that these masses being firmly welded together, deeply imbued with the ideas and spirit of communism, be fully prepared for the communist revolution and the organized construction of life in the new society.

Our road is indeed not a smooth one. We are still faced with many hard tests.

The great cause to the service of which we have voluntarily dedicated ourselves, however, deserves the utmost efforts and sacrifices on our part.

Let us, therefore, make them without any hesitation, profoundly convinced of the inevitable triumph of the international proletarian revolution and of the fact that all mankind will one day be basking in the sun of communism, which is already shining in the *East*, quite close to Lis, over vast Russia peopled with many millions of men, with its wonderful purple rays calling to a new life!

Notes

1. *International,* or *International Workers' Association,* headed by Karl Marx, was founded in 1864.In the declaration of its principles, which became known under the name of Constitutive Manifesto, Marx developed the ideas which had already been exposed in the Communist Manifesto: the International was to be a class organization of the proletariat, fighting for the victory of socialism by wrestling political power from the ruling classes.

2. A General Trade Union Congress was called in Halberstadt om March 14-18, 1892 after the repeat of the exceptional laws against the German socialists. There a general trade union committee under the presidency of Karl Legien was elected, which became the centre of the German trade union movement, as well as a focus of opportunism. The German trade unions pursued a policy of so-called neutrality and were called 'free' trade unions.

3. *Wilhelm II* (1859-1941) - the last German Emperor and Prussian King, a medicore and narrow-minded politician, known for his pompous and megalomaniacal speeches reflecting the aggressive foreign policy of German imperialism. Compelled to abdicate and flee to Holland (November 9, 1918) after the November Revolution in Germany, Wilhelm II later expressed his solidarity with the nazis and in 1940 hailed the invasion of Holland by Hitler's armies.

4. Germany, Germany above all

5. The *American Federation of Labour* (AFL), founded in 1881, compromising mainly the workers' aristocracy under a mercenary clique of revolutionary leaders, such as Gompers up to 1925 (whom Lenin compared to Zubatov), Green and Carey, adopted a hostile attitude to the Russian Revolution. Refusing to join the World Trade Union Federation, it is actively working to split the world trade union movement.

6. *Anarcho-syndicalism* or self-syndicalism - an anarchistic current sprung up in the 80's, which considered trade unions as the only real class organizations, believed solely in the strike weapon as the natural form of class struggle, and was opposed to the political struggle of the proletariat and the dictatorship of the proletariat. Flourishing at the turn of the century, especially in France, Italy and Spain, this current began to decline after the Russian Revolution.

www.ingramcontent.com/pod-product-compliance
Lightning Source LLC
Chambersburg PA
CBHW060017300526
45794CB00003B/1206